THIS BOOK BELONGS TO:

I0772699

ARCANUM

ARCANUM COVER ART

ARCANA MAJORA
0 - Fool

ARCANA MAJORA
VIII – Justice

ARCANA MAJORA

XI - Strength

ARCANA MAJORA
XIII - Death

ARCANA MAJORA
XIV – Temperance

ARCANA MAJORA
XVI - Tower

ARCANA MAJORA

XVII – Star

ARCANA MAJORA

XVIII – Moon

ARCANA MAJORA
XIX - Sun

ARCANA MAJORA

ARCANA MAJORA
XX - JUDGMENT

ARCANA MAJORA

XXI - World

POISONBLADE FAIRY

PUMPKIN WITCH

THREE WITCHES

FUNGAL SHAMAN

GOLDEN POPPY

LADY OF THE WOODS

TRADING CARD DESIGN